TRAGEDY: a tragedy

Will Eno

TRAGEDY: a tragedy

OBERON BOOKS
LONDON

WWW.OBERONBOOKS.COM

First published in 2001 by Oberon Books Ltd.
521 Caledonian Road, London N7 9RH
Tel: +44 (0) 20 7607 3637 / Fax: +44 (0) 20 7607 3629
e-mail: info@oberonbooks.com
www.oberonbooks.com

A catalogue record for this book is available from the British
Library.

ISBN: 978-1-84002-234-6

Printed and bound by CPI Group (UK) Ltd, Croydon, CR0 4YY.

Visit www.oberonbooks.com to read more about all our books
and to buy them. You will also find features, author interviews
and news of any author events, and you can sign up for e-news-
letters so that you're always first to hear about our new releases.

It went down.

— ANONYMOUS

We tried everything.

— ANONYMOUS

Great thanks, great people, near and far

Jack Bradley, Tara Hull, Patrick Dickie, Sue Higginson. And The Gate, The Gate, The Pearly Gate! And the Dark Lady, too.

Gordon Lish, Noy Holland, Sam Michel, Sam Lipsyte, Michael Kimball, David Perry and Joanna P Adler. And the Fair Lady, too.

Contents

INTRODUCTION

Something is on the television, relentlessly. A plane crash, probably. Evening dresses and travel guides washing up on a beach out-of-season. Or, it is one of those new little wars. A scene of an empty street where something important recently happened, a scene of people burning certain flags, waving certain others, or throwing rocks and sticks at a space-age military. Before it all, whatever it is, stands a dashing reporter, talking. Perfectly groomed, dressed in appropriate clothing, properly grave as the moment demands. His teeth are amazing. He shouldn't be there. (Maybe he should be throwing a rock or burning some country's flag. Maybe he could cry. Or help sift through the money and underwear coming in with the tide.) The words flow out of him in local time, keeping time with the urgency or melancholy behind him. Real life on earth, on television. The reporter stands and waits. Then he speaks again. He stands for us, somehow, standing there. He stands for us standing here wondering what we're standing here for. Us, in the wrong place, the wrong time, in a sort of rapture, with life behind us. Us, with only the early technology of our vocabulary, a tongue, trying to identify the rapturous, trying to sum up the miraculous, standing right in front of it. Possibly.

Will Eno
London, 2001

Characters

JOHN IN THE FIELD

FRANK IN THE STUDIO

CONSTANCE AT THE HOME

MICHAEL, LEGAL ADVISOR

THE WITNESS

Setting

The setting is a live television broadcast. Each character is at the place described in his name, except Michael, who is at various locations, and may enter and exit the stage. THE WITNESS will appear with JOHN IN THE FIELD. FRANK IN THE STUDIO sits upstage center. Each speaks as if toward a camera. CONSTANCE AT THE HOME, where noted, turns to address a second camera.

Wardrobe

FRANK IN THE STUDIO might wear a blue suit, white shirt, and red tie. JOHN IN THE FIELD, more casual clothes, a windbreaker, a sport shirt. CONSTANCE AT THE HOME, a skirt-and-jacket suit. MICHAEL, LEGAL ADVISOR, a white shirt and a tie, and perhaps at times a London Fog-style raincoat. THE WITNESS is dressed plainly. All, save THE WITNESS, wear small earphones.

Additional Notes

When in doubt on any point with respect to staging, it may be helpful to refer to a news telecast. Which is not to say that this play is meant primarily as a comment on the news media. It is not.

A reading of *TRAGEDY: a tragedy* was first held at the Royal National Theatre Studio in June 2000. The Gate would like to thank Sue Higginson (Head of Studio) and Jack Bradley (Literary Manager) at the Royal National Theatre for making it possible for *TRAGEDY: a tragedy* to be performed at The Gate.

The production at The Gate Theatre was generously supported by The Jerwood Charitable Foundation: Jerwood Young Designers at The Gate.

For The Gate Theatre:

Artistic Director, Erica Whyman

Producer, Tara Hull

General Manager, Julie Derevycka

Production Manager, Robert Scythes

Technical Manager, Jo Walker

Education Officer, Herta Queirazza

Literary Manager, Kate Wild

Box Office, Paul Long

TRAGEDY: a tragedy was first performed at The Gate Theatre, London, on 5 April 2001, with the following cast:

JOHN IN THE FIELD, Tim Flavin
FRANK IN THE STUDIO, Vincent Marzello
CONSTANCE AT THE HOME, Joanne Mcquinn
MICHAEL, LEGAL ADVISOR, Roderick Smith
THE WITNESS, George Innes

THE TECHNICIAN, Chris Jamba

Director, Paul Miller
Designer, Simon Daw
Lighting Designer, Sarah Gilmartin
Composer/Sound Designer, Dominic Shovelton
Assistant Director, Alex Scrivenor
Assistant Designer, Emmett J. de Monterey
Casting Director, Matt Lesalle
Stage Manager, Maria Dicks
Deputy Stage Manager, Julia Wickham
Voice Teacher, Jeannette Wilson
Photography, Pau Ros
Set Builder, Nigel Parker

The play may begin with a spotlight coming up on FRANK, who begins to speak, and then lights coming up on the other characters, when they make their initial utterance.

It is night.

FRANK IN THE STUDIO

It was quite a day in America, today. The sound of traffic and industry, school bells ringing, life, family life, political life – all the outward signs of a nation's inward vitality, glowing. All lit from above and shined down upon by our long-familiar sun. This is no longer the case. The sun, we understand, has set. Settling through the trees, over a body of water, a few low wispy clouds alit in its final excellent light, and it is gone. For more, we go to John, in the field.

JOHN IN THE FIELD

It's the worst world in the world here tonight, Frank. People are all over, everywhere. Or, they were. Some, hopelessly involved with the grief here at the scene. Still others, passersby to the suffering, slowly passing by, looking, feeling, hoping and believing that they might learn something from these dark times, that they might find some clue about living, hidden in the dusk of the faces of those who have seen so much so fast, and such sadness.

FRANK IN THE STUDIO

The sense of tragedy must be almost palpable there.

JOHN IN THE FIELD

I'm sorry?

He checks his earphone.

FRANK IN THE STUDIO

Is the sense of tragedy palpable?

JOHN IN THE FIELD

Absolutely, Frank. You can feel it. Something is out there, or in here, and this is what we are watching. Or being watched by. One man came by a moment ago, and then, I felt, could not go on. We did all we could to keep him and his hope up until, after a time, his sister arrived, who had seen him wandering on her television, in the background behind me, in her living room at home. When she came and saw him here, she said, "There you are." He smiled. So that was one touching moment in an evening which has been largely bereft of the nice touches normally associated with the soft nights of this season.

CONSTANCE AT THE HOME

I'm here at the home — what? Oh.

JOHN IN THE FIELD

Another thing I should say is, just, what an incredible job the animals have been doing out here tonight. You can perhaps see in my background the dogs going back and forth. They have been barking at the dark and generally doing those things they can usually be counted on to do, and these include: licking hands, yawning, circling before lying down, and making their tags and collars jingle. This, of course, all, as the hours grow more and more late out here, and we, it seems, learn less and less. That's what we know so far. Frank?

FRANK IN THE STUDIO

Thanks, John. Well, we'll be tossing and turning with you, staying right here on top of things, trying to get to the bottom of all this, to find some lesson learned in what has been, so far, a startling unsettling night. Constance? Can you hear me? Constance? Are you there? Well, while we're waiting, perhaps it might make some sense for us —

CONSTANCE AT THE HOME

(*Interrupting.*) Yes, Frank. I'm here at the home of a family we believe may have fallen victim somehow to the event of night, down here, tonight. The scene is quiet. The lights at this simple one-story home are all off. A sprinkler, on a timer, waters the lawn in long even sprinklings of water. The scene is dark. There is, though, in the darkness, a floodlight, activated by a motion detector, periodically flooding the lawn and drive with light. What is felt most here is the mystery. The unspectacular mystery. What remains for us to feel — after having knelt down to feel the worn-out Welcome mat, looked up at the humble shape of a simple house — is, again, the mystery. The feeling that there are deep deep things in the world. Structures, vacancy, departures — and all of the strange sounding names of things, to name only a few.

She turns a quarter turn.

We just a moment ago learned that it was only so long ago that the residents of this modest off-white home gathered on the perfect lawn here, to throw horseshoes and eat food. Also, later that same day, they made a human pyramid. Which, still a little later, in laughter, collapsed. Frank?

FRANK IN THE STUDIO

Thank you, Constance. John?

MICHAEL, LEGAL ADVISOR

It's Michael here, Frank, from the steps of the Capital building. I've just gotten word that we don't know anything more, yet. We are waiting for a disclosure of some sort from someone with, we hope, a clearer understanding of the night, and of the question of liability. We await the comfort of some official language, a smoothly-delivered speech from a sun-tanned man with an easy style and a stunning gold watch. Whereupon, we might be better able to judge whether any of this was justified, and moreover, whether any of this — should it ever end — will ever happen again. And, at the risk of re-stating the obvious —

JOHN IN THE FIELD

(*Interrupting.*) I'm sorry, Michael, John here. Frank, I'm standing next to a man here who happened to be standing right near or somewhere around the horizon as night fell tonight at nightfall.

> *He turns to question THE WITNESS, using a microphone, pausing slightly between each revision of the question.*

Sir, I'm sure you're thinking of home or family
or somewhere else or anything, but just let me
ask you, did you see any sign to foreshadow the
coming dark, anything to indicate that tonight
might be unlike any other in the long and star-
spangled history of night? Some omen? The
famous branch against the window or some
infamous wild animal howl? Did any thing at all
strike you, were you struck by anything striking,
anything...

    He searches for the right word.

striking, as you made your way home from work
today, as the world was turning away from the sun,
and night was starting to settle – or, fall? A piercing
scream, a change in the air, a lack of change, a
sameness? Did you sense any signs like that?

WITNESS

No.

    He pauses and John begins to move
    microphone away from him, and then
    moves it again toward him.

None.

JOHN IN THE FIELD

Frank?

FRANK IN THE STUDIO

Well, certainly, perhaps, one look – if we are
looking closely enough – almost says it all.
Constance, having just heard from the Witness, can
you, from the text of his remarks, and in concert

with what you see there, create a relation that
might help to make this make more sense to us?

A pause.

CONSTANCE AT THE HOME

I'm sorry?

FRANK IN THE STUDIO

A relation.

CONSTANCE AT THE HOME

A relation.

A pause.

FRANK IN THE STUDIO

Yes. A relation. Some relativity. Between the −

MICHAEL, LEGAL ADVISOR

(*Interrupting.*) I'm sorry, Constance, Frank. Michael
here. I've just received a word from the Office
of the Governor and though it helps us gain no
greater insight into the night, it is, I believe, meant
to ease the uneasy nerves of the people of this
state. It reads, "Dear Electorate: A shadow has
crept across the soil of our good state. Day is gone.
It does not, now and perhaps ever, seem to be
coming back. But I beg you, stay calm. No matter
how harsh or Cimmerian the injury or insult to
your person is or may become. Courage, people.
Thank you, the Governor." A word of consolation,
some sentences of hope, a paragraph of words,
on this, our − so far − deepest widest night.
As we move further past dinner and bedtime,

and the darkness which has fallen stays down.
"Cimmerian," I'm told, refers to a people who
were said to live in perpetual night.

Slight pause.

This being a myth, of course. Frank?

FRANK IN THE STUDIO

Thank you, Michael.

Michael exits.

Michael is the station's legal adviser. He —
I understand Constance is standing nearby. Can
you hear —

> *There is static, interference. The lights dim*
> *briefly on Frank. Constance is speaking,*
> *though without sound. The static ends*
> *and we suddenly hear her clearly.*

CONSTANCE AT THE HOME

— the feeling of the feeling that you have been
left behind. In the night, we hear a voice, a father
sitting down to eat, saying grace, or standing at
a door, hat in hand, saying, Good-bye. We hear
children playing, slowly — unsure whether what
can't be seen in the dark will be there again in
the morning. A little girl, a favorite dress. Behind
me, again, a nice house — but no one home. One
wonders where the homeowners went, what they
thought, as they did. Had they some idea, some
inkling, that when havoc was wreaked all over
everything that —

*Static. John's mouth is moving. It ends and
John is clearly audible.*

JOHN IN THE FIELD

— but once was all smiles and sunshine, dear and
wild. And now? Well, the people here have died
down, as all people finally do. But perhaps you
can see in my background the dogs and animal
life. Can what they are doing be called "enduring,"
when they would not call it that, when they don't
even know it's what they're doing? I don't know.
I know that I learned to talk, talking to a dog. A
shepherd/collie mix. She was put to sleep, lain on
a stainless steel table, while all around her a family
wept without understanding. It was a night very
like tonight, except for the obvious difference. But
very much the same. Heartworm, the diagnosis.
The prognosis, nothing. So we're asking that if you
have any rawhide bones or chewy things, please
send them to the station, Attention to me, and they
will be distributed in an equitable and fair —

Static. Same as previous two times.

MICHAEL, LEGAL ADVISOR

(*He enters.*) — whether that is relevant. I can say
that all parties concerned— and this includes
almost everyone — should take great heart in the
kind manner in which most of us, however little
informed, have acted. I am reminded of a favorite
uncle. He gave me a dictionary, which I mistook
as the long sad confusing story of everything. But
he taught me many things about many things. For
example: we put language where loneliness is.
Or for example: while crashing your car, always

steer into the direction of the skid. But now theory must be put into practice, and the stacks of books are pushed aside, as we career heart-first and bookless into the blackening night. My uncle was — well, avuncular is not the wrong word. From the Esplanade, which is empty, this is Michael. Frank.

> *Pause. Frank, not paying attention, is putting eyedrops in his eye.*

As well, we should be grateful that the weather has been so fair, having hindered us not at all, as we seek to make things clear. Frank?

> *Pause. Frank, not paying attention, is putting sugar in his coffee.*

What remains to be seen in this complete darkness is how it will change us. We will suffer consequence. Whenever something happens, so does something else. Frank.

> *Pause. Frank has dropped his pencil and is looking under his desk for it.*

Moreover, and let me add to the above, the sky always has stars in it. It just has to be night-time for us to see them. I was once in a car crash. I forgot to do everything everyone always told me to do. I got a cut on my forehead, over my eye.

> *Pause.*

Frank?

> *Frank is staring off.*

Is he there? Hello. Frank?

FRANK IN THE STUDIO

(*His attention returns.*) Thank you. For that. Yes, I'm
sure you're exactly right. We certainly await an
answer. Meanwhile, we have a recording which
may enlighten the darkness we now inhabit. Let's
have a listen.

> *The tape plays. Possibly the sound of a*
> *light wind blowing, a watery sound, an*
> *old waltz, nothing loud, discernible. All*
> *listen intently. Frank is looking off-stage,*
> *up. The tape plays for a minute or so.*

So there you heard it. There it was. Experts in
these areas will be staring at each other – leaning
forward, their eyebrows raised and with tiny smiles
– listening over and over to see if they might
hear a sound which had not been hitherto heard,
so that they may then attach some meaning to
the – this thus far – nameless experience we now
experience. An investigation is underway, so that
we might put an end and a name to what we in our
simplicity designate as: Night. Any thoughts, John?

JOHN IN THE FIELD

So few, really, Frank.

> *He pauses.*

I think the recording speaks for itself.

> *He pauses.*

In fact, I don't know, I'm sure it does.

FRANK IN THE STUDIO

Michael?

MICHAEL, LEGAL ADVISOR

Legally, it's all allowable, all admissible. Humanly, though, I wonder. Maybe what we heard was the sound of the world kind of "creaking" on its axis. Which I'm told – though there's no evidence to support it – it does. Or maybe it was the leftover hum of some ancient long-dead languages. Or just static.

FRANK IN THE STUDIO

Interesting.

MICHAEL, LEGAL ADVISOR

Were you ever in a crowd of people and you suddenly had the feeling that somebody was about to get hit, hard? That something slow and violent was about to violently and slowly happen. Or, that feeling, if it's flu season, and you suddenly realize you're about to get sick, but you're not sick yet.

FRANK IN THE STUDIO

Michael, I'm going to throw it over to John. John, is our witness still there? Can we get a response from him?

> *THE WITNESS looks slightly confused. JOHN IN THE FIELD holds the microphone up to him. THE WITNESS does not speak.*

JOHN IN THE FIELD

No, Frank. No we can't.

FRANK IN THE STUDIO

And Constance? Constance, are you −

CONSTANCE AT THE HOME

Yes, Frank, I'm here.

She has grass stains on her front.

I think the recording was, in parts, quite beautiful.
After listening, we − the crew out here and I − we
fell down and pounded on the sprinklered earth
here. We did this, perhaps, in hopes that it might
know our sorrow, that the earthly world of worldly
things might feel our suffering, and know our
wonderful physical mystical bodies, which rot.
Listening left us also with the knowledge that, once
you stop to look, everyone has the most beautiful
eyes. Behind me here, the people not here, they
are somewhere else, they are out. One hopes that
they are somewhere together, talking, touching
each other's forearms lightly. It's growing late,
with the lateness informing everything, excepting
ourselves. While, somehow, the night seems to be
getting smarter. And when you listen, the quiet is
not technically that quiet.

Pause.

See? Frank.

FRANK IN THE STUDIO

Thank you, Constance. We are watching and
listening with you, in the same non-silence and
dark. I'm told Michael is standing by with another
word, perhaps another word or two of healing
from the Office of the Governor. Michael?

CONSTANCE AT THE HOME

I'm sorry, Frank. Just one more thing. We –
the crew and I – we just a moment ago saw a
bicycle built-for-two come going by. The two
figures pedaling, one wearing a hat, but neither
responding to our calls. We shined a light at them,
but they kept going. A tandem bicycle at night,
in night. There was a bell on it, possibly shiny,
certainly unrung. Thanks, Frank. Frank, also: a
light rain started. Go ahead, Michael.

FRANK IN THE STUDIO

Thank you, Constance. I'm sorry, Michael. But
we're going now to our national affiliate for an
update as to how this situation affects the country
as a whole. Following this reflection on the nation-
at-large, we will return to our continuing and
hopefully, soon-to-be-over, smaller local coverage.

> *Everyone immediately relaxes. A make-
> up person may attend to CONSTANCE.
> JOHN does some karate, some t'ai chi.
> Frank stands and stretches. MICHAEL
> makes notes. This lasts for about two
> minutes. When FRANK begins again,
> everyone begins to regain his professional
> stance, although one by one, and not all
> at once.*

FRANK IN THE STUDIO

(*Abruptly.*) We're back. Thanks for staying with us.
Word has it there is some word from Constance
out at the home, there, the house with all its lights
out. Constance? Go ahead. What can you tell us?

FRANK removes his earphone to clean it.

CONSTANCE AT THE HOME

(*She is speaking to an unseen crew member, not expecting to be on camera.*) Oh my God, I know. But I really wouldn't know. My first romance was in day camp, so I guess I'm partial to that general time. But then again, my father used to take me with him on walks at night, sometimes. We hear music better at night, did you know that? Because of from when we used to have to listen for the sound of some animal coming out of the dark to kill us by our little fires. So music sounds better when it's dark. Because we're listening for our murderer, an assassin, to rustle somewhere in the leaves and notes.

> *She removes some lint from her jacket. A pause. She listens. She sings very quietly. The first song, "Beethoven's Ninth Symphony/The Ode to Joy." The second, an old drinking song. Frank replaces his earphone.*

Freude, schöner Gotterfunken/ Tochter aus Elysium/ Wir betreten feuertrunken/ Himmlische dein tum-te-dum.

> *Pause.*

Ninety-nine bottles of beer on the wall, ninety-nine bottles of beer, you take one down −

FRANK IN THE STUDIO

(*Interrupting.*) − I'm sorry, Constance?

CONSTANCE AT THE HOME

I'm sorry, Frank.

MICHAEL, LEGAL ADVISOR

It's somehow my fault, Frank. Michael here,
Frank, on the steps of Grange Hall, with, perhaps,
a message of healing – as you said – from the
Governor, I'm not sure. It reads, "Comrades.
Please don't despair overmuch, though the rays
of light are underfew. I, by the way, I write all my
own speeches. By hand. Anyway, maybe it will
only get harder and darker, who's to say? Most
likely, no one. We are individuals in this. But we
are a species, too, and I believe it is time that
we started to act like one, on instinct, in concert,
together, as one, a mob, a community, unruly,
vicious, bloodthirsty, doomed. And if our sun is
dead, then so be it, and in darkness we shall reign
and prosper, until we freeze to death. Drive-in
theaters will thrive, as people picnic in the dark
and eat breakfast by candlelight. Picture it. And
so maybe this is the deal, this picture, that the
sun will just stay down, leaving everything left in
the chaos and obscurity that it was all the time
originally in. Quit asking why it's so dark, and start
remembering how great it was that it ever got light.
Believe you me, if we stay stuck in this fucking
darkness, you won't see me crying. So I say, Let
the looting begin. If you're so afraid, why don't
you panic? This is the night of your lives. If I had
imposed a curfew before, I would lift it now, and
let everybody run wild. Run wild across the world,
lovely people, naked and wild, of flesh torn and
spirit rash. Every night is the dark night of the soul,
but only one can be the darkest, and last. Maybe

we should bring back holding hands. Or maybe a bonfire is in order. In the meantime, watch where you're walking. Keep in touch. Be sweet to yourselves. I'm a ghost. Yours, the Governor." He writes all his own speeches, Frank. All of them, all true, I believe. All written from real life. From his real life. From ours. And by hand. I believe. Frank.

FRANK IN THE STUDIO

Okay, thanks, Michael. Some words, some moving words – even some swear words – from the Governor, clearly shaken by the disaster of night visited upon his fiefdom. Clearly feeling the strain, the pain, the agony of everything, while trying to put his state aright, in some kinder less-harsh light. A man at the brink of everything. Not unlike a lot like all of us. From the beginning, the first thing the first people feared was the dark. Let us not forget that life used to consist of being born, being scared, sleeping on the ground, getting a stick to protect yourself, shaking through the night, deeply ignorant of reality, catching a cold and then dying. And fearing the dark. Perhaps it still does – consist of this. So the Governor is quite right in his noble efforts to embolden us, to buck us up. Constance, any comment?

CONSTANCE AT THE HOME

As for any sign of looting, sanctioned there by the Governor, no, as yet, nothing here, so far. There is no sign of anything else, either.

Pause.

A light rain has stopped. It's quiet still. But still
not silent. But we did spot a horse. I did. A gray
horse. But I guess every horse is black at night. He
wanted water, I felt. I tried to hit him with a rock.
I don't know why or what I was doing. Maybe
it was my…due to some ancient long dead…
certainly the horsie never…I don't know. I hit
him in the eye, it sounded like. He galloped away.
Neighing and whinnying. Crying. Oh, one more
thought —

> *She stops.*

> *A pause.*

FRANK IN THE STUDIO

Constance?

> *CONSTANCE AT THE HOME turns
> to address her second camera, but does not
> say anything.*

FRANK IN THE STUDIO

Constance!

CONSTANCE AT THE HOME

(*Patiently.*) I heard you the first time, Frank.

FRANK IN THE STUDIO

Well, then shouldn't you have —

MICHAEL, LEGAL ADVISOR

(*Interrupting.*) Perhaps she should have, Frank.
Frank, it's Michael here, Frank. It is my feeling,
Frank, based on an analysis of the Governor's

letters, that things are getting serious, and if they were serious before, then they are more so now, and if they were more so before, then, now, Jesus, Frank, it might be safe to say that they are awful. Hopeless, more or less. *Mas o menos, en Espagnol,* for those people tonight who are listening in Spanish. Frank?

> *Exits.*

FRANK IN THE STUDIO

(*Irked.*) Okay, Michael. Thank you for that opinion.

> *Pause.*

Many of our listeners are, perhaps, yes, Spanish, tonight. Every night, I suppose. So, *Beunas Noches,* to them.

> *Brief pause.*

Why don't we go now to good old John, who is afield. He covered the race for Governor all last year and may have therefore heard more fully the message we all just only partly heard. John? Okay, John. Go ahead. John.

JOHN IN THE FIELD

(*He is holding some papers. He looks at them, and then looks away. He speaks slowly.*) In the interim, I, somewhat out of – Somewhat out of what? The Governor's right, Frank. Everyone's right, whatever everyone means – stuck with saying, as everyone is, only the words they already know. Such as the words, I'm dizzy. Or the words, I keep looking for something to look at. Or such as, If

I closed my eyes, I know I would get sick. Such
as I hear the sound of O-negative blood sloshing
through me. Such as, I'm alone in this body, and
it isn't on my side. Such as I want my mother here
more than everything. Such as, But if she were to
come, I would ask her to leave. Such as, Frank?
Or, slosh.

>   *Pause.*

I think I have heartworm. It's always night, but,
sometimes, it's day. That makes sense, doesn't
it? Maybe you can see in my background…my
shadow. I miss what I used to think about. The
love of a young mother and father, when they were
young and loving. Spoons and knives, mirrors,
braces, everything – all the glittery things of a
well-lit civilization. And riding bikes around. And
a dog at a door. A good good sunny dog. All this.
Everywhere you look, you see your life, no longer
there. And if it's dark, well, then, then what?
Frank?

>   *A pause.*

FRANK IN THE STUDIO

Okay, John. Yes, well – Certainly –

(*Quietly.*) That was John in the field. John, out
there, somewhere – reckoning. Trying like all of
us to find some way of defining the evening we
currently reside in now. Or, I suppose I mean
night, and not evening. And, are occupied by, and
not, reside in. It is difficult to find the right – We
thank you for – Let's go now –

>   *He looks at the floor. Pause.*

35

CONSTANCE AT THE HOME

Frank?

Pause.

Frank.

FRANK IN THE STUDIO

(*He looks up.*) Constance?

CONSTANCE AT THE HOME

Yes, Frank. I'm sorry about singing, earlier. I hope John is okay. He will be. I hope. But, Frank, how are you? Do you need air or anything? Water? Anything, you know, elemental? Because we've, at least, we've all been standing around outside somewhere, and at least the dark we're in is real. You've had to stay at that desk all this time, sitting with yourself in the artificial light. It must be hard.

JOHN IN THE FIELD appears sick.

FRANK IN THE STUDIO

I'm fine. Not so hard. But thank you, though, for thinking of me. Maybe I should take a little walk. Now that I start to think, I think I might be overworked. Or sick with something. And John's last report didn't do much to lighten or lift my spirit. The air is very –

Pause.

The light is very bright.

CONSTANCE AT THE HOME

Oh, Frank. Here I am, about to say the wrong thing to say. Maybe it's not the time or the place, but when is it ever, and where? Never, nowhere. But, sometimes, when you sign off and say goodnight, it sounds so sad. Whatever words you say, the sound of your voice says, "Good night, Farewell, Be Well, We're all going to die, Please be nice, and, Please, I don't want to have to hear any more news until I have to." I look at the lines of ink going into the pocket of your shirt. Your eyes look tired. You wash your shirt from that day, at night, in the clean kitchen light. This is long after all the news is over, and your back hurts. Then you try sitting different ways, in different chairs. I don't know if you're the crying kind. Then you have a glass of milk. Frank?

FRANK IN THE STUDIO

(*He appears moved.*) Thank you, Constance. It's nice to be imagined. Doing anything, even if it's only laundry. Which, incidentally, I send out. But thank you.

> *He pauses, looks at some papers on his desk.*

We go to Michael. Michael?

MICHAEL, LEGAL ADVISOR

(*Enters.*) Frank, I'm here at the First Congregational Church, Frank, where no one has gathered. First this, briefly, from the Governor,

> *He reads.*

"I am toying with the idea of declaring a state of emergency; although at this point in my life, I feel it would be a great redundancy." Secondly, Frank, I always pictured you coming home late to your house, home to some thing that you loved more than anything. Maybe music or scratchy records of famous speeches. You sit and listen until almost when the paper is delivered. There are photographs lining the staircase you don't climb. You look at your books. Then you have a glass of milk. Thirdly, Frank, we have, statistically speaking, every reason to expect night to end. But, in another way of speaking, we don't. Either way, statistically speaking, thanks a lot for all the times when, when I first got to the station, you used to always wave me over to sit with you at lunch. That was really nice. Thanks, Frank. Also, again, it's dark out tonight. You can't really see anything. Frank?

He exits.

FRANK IN THE STUDIO

Thank you, Michael. And you're welcome.

He is regaining his composure.

Well. A night, increasingly and ultimately, of gratitude, as we all stare straightly into the face of that thing which has been staring out at us, all this time. There's a certain –

JOHN IN THE FIELD

(*Interrupting. Anxious.*) Frank! I'm sorry!

(*Apologetic.*) I'm sorry, Frank.

FRANK IN THE STUDIO

Yes, John? What is it?

JOHN IN THE FIELD

Nothing, Frank.

FRANK IN THE STUDIO

It seemed like something.

JOHN IN THE FIELD

I know, it did, didn't it? I don't know. Go ahead.

FRANK IN THE STUDIO

There's certainly a very definite –

JOHN IN THE FIELD

Frank! I'm sorry, again. It's this, again. It's physical. This is this, Frank. John, here. I feel sick and weak, and sick. It's my heart.

(*He whispers.*) My fucking cunt heart.

(*Regular voice.*) I hear it. I forget to breathe while I listen and there's nothing to look at to stop me from listening. Systole, diastole, systole. The same old story. I can't breathe. Or I feel like I can't. My heart sounds different. From me. I'm worried. John, here. There's some owl or something out there. Some sound that sounds like that recording. But there's no star, there's no manger, no blazing charioteer. I don't mean to get religious, but what am I supposed to do? I feel faint. It's dark. My legs are shaky. Am I faint? Frank?

(*He is hyperventilating.*) It's dark out. Perhaps you can see – Can what we are doing be called – What do I say, Frank? Faint? Shaky?

FRANK IN THE STUDIO

(*He doesn't know how to help.*) It's okay, John. John, it's all right. Just – it's okay, John.

CONSTANCE AT THE HOME

Frank, if I could?

FRANK IN THE STUDIO

Please, Constance. Of course you can. Yes, you go ahead.

CONSTANCE AT THE HOME

Thank you, Frank. Breathing is the first thing, John. John, just be yourself, and breathe. There's something in the atmosphere tonight, besides just the night, adding a little mystery to life's ambiguity, and making it harder to breathe. There's a weight.

Pause.

Moments ago, John, a car came by. We saw it coming, and then heard the radio in it go past, and then it drove off, people inside, over the curvature of the earth. There was a dog with his head out the window, loving life. I know you like dogs. I don't know if I'm helping. Darkness is always coming, from somewhere, for somebody, somewhere else. The wee hours ever approach, and everyone's afraid, and they run, or go to sleep, and this is our life, and the race is on. No one yelled Ready,

Set, Go. Or, Lights, Places, Action! No one yelled
anything. To think of the world, and us trying to
hold on. No wonder you're dizzy. It's dark inside
of us; I mean that as no metaphor. Have yourself
looked at by someone. Then look back at them.
Try to envision anything good, John. Frank?

FRANK IN THE STUDIO

Thank you, Const –

JOHN IN THE FIELD

(*Interrupting.*) Thanks, Constance.

MICHAEL, LEGAL ADVISOR

(*He enters.*) That was nice, Constance. You know,
John, sometimes if I'm not feeling well, I lie down.
And if that doesn't work, I try to stand up, or sit.

JOHN IN THE FIELD

Thanks, Michael. I'll try that.

FRANK IN THE STUDIO

And also, John, you know, when tough times
come, I'll occasionally – apparently – have a glass
of milk.

MICHAEL, LEGAL ADVISOR

Excuse me, everyone. A communiqué, from
here at the Reservoir. I've just been informed
that the Governor has run away. Here follows a
final unperfumed letter he left, before adjourning
a meeting in the statehouse and climbing out a
window and sliding down a drain pipe. "Good

People. It's likely going to be all right. You might be going to be fine. Thank you for your confidence, which I will now betray. You deserved more and better. I looked into myself. I did some soul searching but didn't find anything. If it makes you feel better, I was going to die anyway. Bye now, the erstwhile governor, your governor, The Governor." At the bottom, a thumbprint. Half a drawing of an elephant. He's gone. He was…

Pause.

helpful, I thought. To me. Back to you.

He exits.

FRANK IN THE STUDIO

History seems to be – I don't know – everything seems to be making history tonight. Dark times call for dark people. This is history, indeed, in fact. We are there, here. And I should think we should feel blessed to be witness to all this. Speaking of the same, how's our witness out there, John?

JOHN IN THE FIELD

Here he is here, Frank.

John holds his microphone up to the WITNESS, who looks at it, and then John.

WITNESS

I have heart –

Pause. He clears his throat.

I have heart trouble in my family, too. I don't eat any salt.

JOHN IN THE FIELD

Right.

Pause.

Go light on the salt. Frank?

FRANK IN THE STUDIO

Thanks, John. We might remind everyone to –

CONSTANCE AT THE HOME

I'm sorry, Frank. But this just in, which may shed a little you-know-what on matters. We've discovered a note out here at the house I'm at, or, standing out in front of. Held down by a few pebbles, out back here on the deck, small, white, written in a writing now running with the weight and dew of the night. Whether it is in a woman's hand or a man's hand, we cannot tell, but it is recognizably human handwriting. It reads: "Hey you – How are things? I waited and then I left. Let's try and talk this week. Come over and let's listen to music. I hope I see you soon. Isn't the sky strange? I have to run. Guess who I ran into today? Call me. Sincerely, Me." Plainspoken, and to-the-point, written in a loopey American calligraphy, lying here amidst the grass slowly growing in the night. Something illuminating should be said. What, I don't know.

FRANK IN THE STUDIO

Constance, any ideas as to who might have written it, and what it might have meant?

A pause.

CONSTANCE AT THE HOME

I'm sorry, Frank – I wasn't listening.

FRANK IN THE STUDIO

Don't you have an earphone on?

CONSTANCE AT THE HOME

I do. But I was listening to something else.

FRANK IN THE STUDIO

I thought it was quiet where you were.

CONSTANCE AT THE HOME

It is. But I was thinking.

A pause.

FRANK IN THE STUDIO

About what?

CONSTANCE AT THE HOME

Nothing. I don't know. Myself, and that horse. Everything. My girlhood. What I did with boys. About coming home when there was no one home. And how a certain life kept coming at me, which was mine. And how now I have to live it, as me. Because why? Because of some little thing that I saw when I was little? A glint on some car keys, or a pattern on a sunny rug, to which I mistakenly attached some mistaken little meaning? So now my life lives itself out, in revisions of revisions of something that was blurry to begin with? I wish that note were for me. I quote, "Let's talk this week. Come over, for music." Or whatever it said. That was the nicest thing I've ever read. And, I feel, the most —

She pauses, stops.

A pause.

FRANK IN THE STUDIO

The writing was, yes, it was wonderfully readable writing. It would make anyone feel good to have been written that. Thank you, Constance. Meanwhile, I'm sorry, we return again now to national coverage for another word on the larger story of the story of our nation in night.

There is a difference from the earlier break. There is little activity. MICHAEL enters. Generally, everyone stares ahead for about a minute.

FRANK IN THE STUDIO

Apparently, there's trouble with a transmitter somewhere. We'll have something for you soon. Michael, do you suppose —

MICHAEL, LEGAL ADVISOR

(*He interrupts.*) This is Michael at the White House, saying, *Esta Miguel a la Casa Blanca,* here with a few more bloodless fruitless legalisms to offer. No official word, but we will keep waiting. Born to wait, wonder, and die, were we. By the way, is it dark enough for you? Can you see me okay? Darling? And what's that word that means crepuscular? Or is it just crepuscular? My love, my life! Let us convene in a dry and golden wheat field, where I, on bended knee, will then proclaim that this is Michael, on bended knee, in a dry and golden wheat field. Frank?

FRANK IN THE STUDIO

Michael, who are you talking to?

MICHAEL, LEGAL ADVISOR

Not to be difficult, but I think you mean, To whom may I say I am speaking. And I don't know, Frank. And the Shadow doesn't know. And I don't know. Legally. But I look out and see this is real, something real is coming; possibly, nothing good; certainly, not anything easy. No. Theoretically, into this exact world, I should have never been born.

CONSTANCE AT THE HOME

(*The following exchanges move quickly.*) Michael.

FRANK IN THE STUDIO

Jesus.

MICHAEL, LEGAL ADVISOR

Mr Governor, a question in the back.

JOHN IN THE FIELD

John?

FRANK IN THE STUDIO

John. Everyone.

CONSTANCE AT THE HOME

It may be untimely of me to say, but, recently,
I heard a hot-air balloon going by. Floating,
overhead, in the dark. That is a curious reaction
to things, to go ballooning. Everyone?

MICHAEL, LEGAL ADVISOR

In many ways, I'm floating overhead, in the dark.
In many other ways, everything I've ever said was
untimely of me to say.

FRANK IN THE STUDIO

People, please.

JOHN IN THE FIELD

Frank, it's night. Also, I think I may be having a
stroke. Or something very personal like that. Back
to you, Frank. Or should I say, Back to you, Frank.

FRANK IN THE STUDIO

It is indeed. And we −

MICHAEL, LEGAL ADVISOR

The Governor, he gone. They ain't no moon no
more. Nothing shining anymore from on high to
down upon our dull and raggedy procession. Deep
deep black.

JOHN IN THE FIELD

This is John, crapping out.

CONSTANCE AT THE HOME

Hello. Has the word dusk been used, yet?

FRANK IN THE STUDIO

Yes, in fact, since you ask. I think, once.

CONSTANCE AT THE HOME

I thought, once. I just saw, I alone, I just saw something I thought was a person, whirling in the wind. But it was only a person's clothing, hanging on a clothesline, whirling in the wind. A common mistake. Anyone?

FRANK IN THE STUDIO

All right, Constance. Maybe it might be best for us to try to hear a little more on the political situation. Michael?

MICHAEL, LEGAL ADVISOR

There's no political situation anymore. And I think we've heard enough name calling for tonight. If I may be frank.

JOHN IN THE FIELD

A person is not a person's name. I was such a baby when I was born. We had an important dog when I was little. I named it something, some name, and that is what it answered to, its whole life, until it went deaf, or didn't answer anymore, and then died, or, started shivering, and then died. But that's what happens.

CONSTANCE AT THE HOME

I don't mind mine. But it isn't the most popular name in the world: Constance. Frank was very popular at one time. Frank?

FRANK IN THE STUDIO

Yes thank you. Frank is a fairly popular name.
But I'll try again, any word from the lieutenant
governor? Is a swearing-in on the horizon?

MICHAEL, LEGAL ADVISOR

(*In mock exasperation.*) Frank, Frank, Frank, Frank.
Frank?

He exits.

FRANK IN THE STUDIO

Okay, Michael, very good. John, please, who
would take over for the Governor, here?

JOHN IN THE FIELD

Who knows, Frank. Not me. Not any animals,
either. For the animals are gone, having scampered
off, as all animals finally do. Leaving here, quiet. I
wish I had something real to tell you. I don't know.

Pause. In a higher voice.

Can't anyone in this family talk? I am not your
maid! I am a sixty-eight year old woman. I was
quite a looker in my day, but now I stare out a
window. My son's name is John. He works for the
news. He was born with a murmur. He gets his
eyes from his father and me. He reads to our dog.

Pause.

Would you listen to me? I'm starting to sound like
my mother. What am I starting to look like?

FRANK IN THE STUDIO

Sit down, John. Slow down, John.

CONSTANCE AT THE HOME

Everything is speeding up – to no end, but just faster. Speaking of ancestry, my father, now dead, is quite a talker. Always a story, some quote. But he's neither here nor there. But nothing is coming riding by. But the note is lost or blown away. Likewise, the balloonists. The sprinklers, off, as strangely as they came on. There is a seashell from some sea lying in this yard. It does not look serious. I – on the other hand – I feel I do. Frank, would you say that you'd say that I was a beautiful and serious woman?

A pause.

FRANK IN THE STUDIO

Constance. I –

CONSTANCE AT THE HOME

(*Interrupting.*) I thought so.

MICHAEL, LEGAL ADVISOR

(*He enters.*) Sorry to interrupt. The barrister, here, here on the surface of Earth. They should have never let me use the alphabet. This is a difficult case. But, the defense rests. But, there is no defense. The court, which is a joke, is adjourned. I've weighed both sides very carefully and now I believe I have enough information to completely give up. Maybe the Governor never said anything. It's too late for me to tell. The fact-finding is over.

And everyone files out saying, No comment. Files out, not even saying, No comment.

A pause.

FRANK IN THE STUDIO

Michael? Michael! John, please tell us —

JOHN IN THE FIELD

(*His face is bloodied.*) The news is no more newsworthy from here, Frank. The apple doesn't fall very far, Frank. Am I omitting some part of the expression? Frank? Gentleman Franklin? Deuxieme francs. Do you have any birthmarks, Frank? I once knew someone. Going to the beach is fun. We stopped seeing each other. I hope she's dead. She had light blonde hair and light blue eyes. She was American, which is a beautiful word. We met at an animal rescue league. I am making incredible sense. To rephrase that, I hope she is alive.

In his monitor, Frank sees John's bloody face. He interrupts him.

FRANK IN THE STUDIO

John, my God. Are you all right? What happened?

JOHN IN THE FIELD

(*Touching his hand to his face and then looking at his hand, he realizes his nose is bleeding.*) My nose is bleeding.

FRANK IN THE STUDIO

Can you get a handkerchief or anything to stop the blood?

JOHN IN THE FIELD

(*Amiably.*) "Stop the bleeding," is that your advice?

>*Brief pause.*

(*Awkwardly.*) I'm sorry, I don't know what I was saying before.

>*Brief pause.*

(*Confidently.*) Oh, right – I remember. I hope she is alive. She is forever in my heart, which is broken, and has been since birth. She was, of course, an earthling. I, for instance, went to school. Does anyone else miss anyone? Is there a sister from somewhere, coming? I am wandering through life on a television in someone's living room. Perhaps you can't see, just over my shoulder, anything. And I'm bleeding. And I'm saying, "I'm bleeding." I am sick and signing off. Off into the – what would be a beautiful word?

>*He tilts his head back to stop the bleeding, looking straight up.*

CONSTANCE AT THE HOME

I hit a horse with a rock. It's bleeding somewhere, too, looking up, an animal. Nothing else. Except, there is a ceramic rabbit on the lawn out back. A pretty ceramic rabbit, with one ear broken off. Nothing else. Except, there is a ceramic deer, three legs and a crack in its head. The floodlight that goes on when it senses any motion hasn't gone on for the longest time. All this ceramic wildlife, and, me, the most ceramic of all, here amidst —

FRANK IN THE STUDIO

(*Interrupting.*) In our continuing effort to keep you informed, we now go to the Emergency Broadcasting Network. The years of testing are over, the phrase "an actual emergency," now a reality. And, we go, now.

> *A problem. There is nothing. No sound, nothing.*

Obviously, more technical trouble. We hope to have that for you, as soon as possible.

> *Pause.*

Constance, are you there? We will get you that message as soon as we can. Constance, I'm sorry I interrupted you. I know you can hear me. I hear you breathing.

> *Pause. Constance is standing, frozen. John has his head tilted upward. Michael is looking down.*

Anybody? John. People, everybody, please.

> *Long pause.*

If I can keep going, then anyone can. It is nighttime, so we pray for morning. Should morning come, we pray for afternoon, and then, by then, for night. This is the natural ritual. People! Somebody answer! Would somebody come out of nowhere and interrupt?! Is there a responsive person anywhere? Could someone tell me, in whatever words, in any language whatsoever, some story of local human interest? Some global event or a little story about the re-naming of a street, or something funny someone did in school today, so that the world and this broadcast do not fall further apart. Now!? Could one of you please report a little lie for me to live by? Could somebody help me? Does not one of you realize what it means for me to ask that!? To talk like this?

A pause.

CONSTANCE AT THE HOME

I don't know, Frank.

JOHN IN THE FIELD

I don't know, either.

MICHAEL, LEGAL ADVISOR

I know.

FRANK IN THE STUDIO

Yes? Michael?

A pause.

MICHAEL, LEGAL ADVISOR

I don't know, Frank.

FRANK IN THE STUDIO

Well. How unknowing of everyone. "In the lawnmowing tones of speeches unspoke, in a light wholly absent, by a river by a willow, there did the

dark horses of the thrashing — " Forget it. I don't
have the time or breath to misquote old poetry.

Pause.

Jesus.

He checks his pulse.

My heart is going — John, please, anyone, I think I
might be having — John, tell me now, what did you
do to ease your heart, before?

JOHN IN THE FIELD

I was lying, before.

FRANK IN THE STUDIO

You weren't having trouble?

JOHN IN THE FIELD

No, I was. I really was. I was lying, just then.

FRANK IN THE STUDIO

(*Deep breaths. Takes some pills. He recovers, somewhat.
The next line, sharply.*) Well, thank you, son, for
your honesty. Constance, be daughterly with me.
Maybe you could describe your environment, out
there. Even, whatever season we are in. You don't
have to make sentences. You could give us a list.
A nice list to relax us. Are there daffodils?
Or snowbanks? Are there geese, flying in any
direction?

A pause.

CONSTANCE AT THE HOME

There is some −

FRANK IN THE STUDIO

Yes?

CONSTANCE AT THE HOME

I'm not finished.

FRANK IN THE STUDIO

Of course, I'm sorry. Go ahead.

CONSTANCE AT THE HOME

− fog.

FRANK IN THE STUDIO

A blinding fog, is it? What would you say our visibility is? Our visibility must be practically zero.

CONSTANCE AT THE HOME

Enough. No more, Frank. Please don't speak to me like that anymore.

Pause.

That's all. Except, my father liked horses. Except, I saw one. I'm a terrible person. But, who isn't? Not me. No wonder everyone is never home. No wonder it's just the remains, by the time I always get there.

She turns to her second camera.

I deserve nothing, and I thank you all for giving me it.

FRANK IN THE STUDIO

Constance, I don't think that's true. You —

CONSTANCE AT THE HOME

Spare me your thoughts on what you do not think is true.

MICHAEL, LEGAL ADVISOR

Michael here, Frank.

FRANK IN THE STUDIO

Yes?

> *A pause. MICHAEL, LEGAL ADVISOR, says and does nothing.*

JOHN IN THE FIELD

A vacuum, how perfect. When I was six, this was fairly impressive: A, B, C, D, E, F, G — ah, but I'm sure you know how all that turns out. This concludes myself. You?

FRANK IN THE STUDIO

Okay, John, let us —

JOHN IN THE FIELD

No. Let us not. This is fake. Mum is the word. Let us be mum, for so are the gods. Hi Mum. I quit. Go to someone else. Roll some video of a family at the beach. Or a limp flag in the historical sun. Cut away from me. Go to black. I am.

> *A pause.*

FRANK IN THE STUDIO

John, what about all your stately animals? And the news on that lone man who was walking around, with the sister who came in from home? Don't we have a duty? At least, a curiosity? I know we are all very tired.

JOHN tilts his head back.

MICHAEL, LEGAL ADVISOR

Michael, from here on the mis-steps of my life, Frank. Legally, everybody is going to be dead. Legally, everybody leaves you. I should. But I'll stay. But I don't think I should say anything. I don't think I read the dictionary closely enough. I don't think I did anything closely enough.

CONSTANCE AT THE HOME

As for here, there isn't anyone here. The point is finally driven home, at this empty house. The grass will yellow, then blacken. The house will rot, the driveway crumble, the sprinklers freeze. The human pyramid will collapse, still a little later, in laughter. Girls will die, Frank.

Pause.

I think I have something stuck in my eye. And something else stuck in my throat. And my life is stuck in my body, which they will stick in the earth. Everywhere I look are signs of people having left. Was I born to stand outside, talking about inside? I give up. I can't keep up with all the leaving people. With the fucking thinking and speaking. I'm sorry. Frank, I'm sorry for swearing.

It won't happen again. Nothing will. I pictured it differently. I'm sorry.

FRANK IN THE STUDIO

Constance? John. I am calling anyone's name.

A long long pause. Clearly no one else is going to speak.

When I was younger – Years back, when I used to – People have sometimes asked – or, to do –

Pause.

To do this job was always my dream. To be trusted and turned to and believed in. For years of weekdays, I grew, and felt myself growing, to become all of those things above. But I am not one. I didn't anchor anything. I get older, every weeknight, without change. The flashlight is dead and we are left darkling – as we used to say in my youth, which is also gone, with no remains.

WITNESS

(*A long pause. He steps into John's position, looking at and around the "camera."*) Is all this still on? Hi, Frank? I'm that witness that John out here interviewed earlier. I've been standing here listening (*He motions toward "camera."*), through the thing on the thing here. Listen, I think you're great at what you do. You seem really nice. Constance, if you can hear this, I love you, I watch you all the time. And John out here is the best. I remember once he covered some storm in a raincoat, live. And Michael, on the steps of all-over, talking about the legality of things. Everyone is great. Everyone should keep going. We listen for you.

We are listening. Frank works so hard. Come on. Everyone is watching and waiting, all these people, leaned-forward, real leaning people, watching and listening.

A pause.

FRANK IN THE STUDIO

It seems there is no word.

WITNESS

I guess not. I can say what I saw, tonight. I'm not seasoned, or eloquent, like John and them. But I was standing around. It was practically twilight. This is my custom. A plane went flying by, a plane did, and made a trail across the sky. I stared. Like this. A dog barked at something. Someone was teaching a baby how to walk on the sidewalk. Lights started coming on, with people coming home. And all this stuff, this whole neighborhood of stuff, I saw. I heard a band practicing, keeping starting over with the same song. I don't ever remember feeling exactly like I felt. There were some birds in a tree, finishing up singing. Someone came walking by with a garbage bag. I smelled the ocean, which we live nowhere anywhere near. I thought about an ocean. Bugs banged against the outdoor lights. It felt suddenly really sad, I felt, but also not sad, looking at the street in that light. Then, I heard someone calling somebody's name for them to come in and eat. And then, night fell, like usual. But differently,
sort of.

Pause.

That's all, from what I saw. It would be like that, at the start of the end of the world, I guess, wouldn't it. This is all. I thought it was pretty. But what do I know? Except all that.

FRANK IN THE STUDIO

Thank you. Thanks. The night has produced an eloquent man.

THE WITNESS

Well, I don't know. I heard words around the house, you know? Who knows.

FRANK IN THE STUDIO

Yes.

Pause. He is nodding off.

I'm listening, I'm sorry. I'm very tired. I'm not well. I…

(*He whispers.*) Jesus, Jesus. Ironic, my awakening in life would happen at night, with me having grown so tired, so sleepy and sick of it all.

THE WITNESS

I know.

He doesn't understand the irony.

The irony.

Pause.

Frank, once I saw the Governor in person. He was filling his car up with gas. He was wearing shorts and sunglasses.

Frank doesn't respond. He is clearly exhausted.

True.

Pause.

How about – well, no, that's no good.

Pause.

If I ever asked for a story at night, either my mother or father always told me this one. Let's see. Once there was a world and it had, you know, everything in the world in it. Rocks, trees, oceans, animals, people, houses, governments. All of it. It was great, everyone thought and felt. Then everyone started to imagine it getting ruined and run down. And that started happening in reality. People started hurting and killing everyone. But then this boy or girl was born that everyone loved due to their beauty. And the child said to everyone, "I would be scared, too." So everyone was scared together.

FRANK puts his head down.

And all their worries turned into a sort of comfort. And their doubts about things turned into a kind of faith, sort of. And new people were born during this. And new words were invented to talk about people with. Newness, like, reigned over the world in the story. Then a bright white horse showed up. I don't know why or what happened with it or any of the rest of it, because I always fell asleep.

FRANK appears asleep.

At the end, though, I bet my mother or father whispered, Sweet Dreams.

Brief pause.

I can almost see them, leaning over and pulling the sheet up and whispering something simple like that over me in my dark room. Good night, Sweet Dreams, someone is whispering over me, because they loved me and it is night-time and they wanted to try to say something.

(*Softly.*) Frank?

Pause.

Goodnight, Sweet dreams, they whisper, and then walk backwards out the door, and close it.

Light fades.

The End.

OTHER WILL ENO TITLES